THE 4 STEPS

A PRACTICAL GUIDE TO BREAKING THE ADDICTIVE CYCLE

A.D. BURKS

The 4 STEPS: A Practical Guide to Breaking the Addictive Cycle

I have tried to recreate events, locales and conversations from my memories of them. In order to maintain their anonymity in some instances I have changed the names of individuals and places. I may have changed some identifying characteristics and details such as physical properties, occupations and places of residence.

The 4 STEPS: A Practical Guide to Breaking the Addictive Cycle
Copyright © 2016 by A.D. Burks

All rights reserved. No part of this publication may be reproduced, stored in a retrieval system or transmitted in any form or by any means, electronic, mechanical, photocopying, recording or otherwise, without the prior written permission of the publisher.

ISBN 13: 978-0983849940
ISBN-10: 0983849943

Published by: Burloc Media Group
Houston, TX

First Edition January 2016

Cover Design by: Albert Reef
Interior Layout by: Margie Baxley
Editing by: August Tarrier, Ph.D.

Printed in the United States of America

Table of Contents

Introduction 8
STEP 1: Re/Establish Your Relationship with God 17
STEP 1 QUESTIONS 35
Trust and Commitment 36
Sin 41
Pain 46
Happiness Vs. Joy 50
Living With A Purpose 54
Forgiveness 62
STEP 2: Abstinence 69
STEP 2 QUESTIONS 83
Abstinence 84
Food, Prescription Drugs, Sex, and Other Addictions .. 87
Forced, Self-Imposed or Chosen 92
The Challenge 103
Making a Decision 107
STEP 3: Change Your Environment: Walk Away from Your Triggers 115
STEP 3 QUESTIONS 130
Who 128
Why, What and When 133
Shame 138
People Pleasing and Rejection 142
Hopelessness 149

An Impossible Dream 152
Not Getting Your Way 159
How 164
STEP 4: Establish a Support Network 171
   STEP 4 QUESTIONS 190
      Spirituality 186
      Addiction-Free 190
      Being Unselfish 194
      Honesty 199
      Trustworthiness 204
      Being Protective 208
      Empathy 211
      Integrity 214
      Accountability 217
      Resourcefulness 220
Conclusion 225
Acknowledgements 231

Introduction

I'd like to be the first to commend you for taking the most important STEP towards breaking your addictive cycle—**seeking a way out.** As someone who struggled with sex addiction for nearly twelve years, I can both sympathize and empathize with what you are going through: I cycled in and out of addiction, continually thinking I could stop whenever I wanted but ultimately finding myself right back where I started, in a place of indescribable pain and loneliness. But YOU, and not anyone else, have made the choice that enough is enough, and YOU are ready to break YOUR addictive cycle once and for all.

Addiction = Pain

At the root of any addiction is pain. It doesn't matter whether you're addicted to drugs, alcohol, sex, food, gambling, shopping or any combination of those or anything else; once you delve below the surface of the addiction(s) what you'll find is unaddressed pain. In order to function and protect ourselves we put up walls that make it extremely difficult to figure out what is causing our true source(s) of pain. Why the walls? **Fear!**

Introduction

Everyone wants **Love**. We fear that if we really address the pain at the root of our addiction, we'll no longer be loved—by those we love, those who love us or anyone whose love we want. We've all come to accept that "real" love is based on conditions, but that is not love. Sadly, our addictive mind feeds into this myth.

Real love is unconditional! Nothing you can say, think, do or not do will make someone who really loves you stop loving you. In reality, we base love on conditions; we all do it—the people who say they love us and those we say we love. So it is difficult to really love unconditionally; if we did, we wouldn't withhold our love when someone else acts in ways that we don't agree with. Because we all have to keep our world running smoothly and maintain the perception that we are loved, we hide the pain behind walls and let our addiction(s) help us manage the pain.

Often we aren't able to accept unconditional love because we don't love ourselves unconditionally. We tell ourselves that we'll finally love ourselves unconditionally once a certain set of conditions is established: when we improve how we look, make more money, buy a certain car or house, land a job in the right field, become friends with a certain person or get married to the perfect spouse—in short, when we have finally arrived. But what happens once we achieve those goals and we still feel unloved? Or what happens if we never achieve them? Would

9

our lives had been a waste or would we have lived in pain all the time, chasing what we felt would make us feel love?

By basing love on achieving those goals we are once again placing conditions on love. And what's worse is that those conditions aren't external conditions set by others—these are conditions we set for ourselves. While we may believe we can change another person via force or through manipulation (tools addicts use to feel a sense of control and power, but which only serve to feed the addiction), in fact this is not true. Here's the blessing, though: if we invest that same energy into loving ourselves, we won't need to try to force someone else to love us, because we love ourselves. When we are able to love ourselves unconditionally, we won't feel the need to change ourselves when others don't love us unconditionally. So why don't we truly love ourselves?

We've been told both directly and indirectly that we aren't worthy of love just as we are. This message comes from the people who love us, those who we love, or who we think love us, or who say they love us, or maybe they don't even know us or they outright hate us. The message takes root in the addict's mind and is continuously played out at an unconscious level, making us act out. Let's say it plainly: that message is a lie. Every single person is worthy of unconditional love—especially addicts. Let me say it another way: at the lowest point in your life, no matter what you did or did not do, you are worthy of being loved. Once you know this for yourself and it is ingrained in your mind and spirit, you'll be able to start the healing process. Once an addict is able to change his or her mindset, to feel worthy of unconditional love, and to understand that message deep in his or her spirit, the addiction loses its power. But if someone does not believe that the Source of Love, which I call God, loves them unconditionally, the task can seem impossible. Why would an all-loving God fail to extend love to a person who He took time to place on this earth for a specific purpose? Or rather, why would someone think and feel they could do something to make God stop loving them?

The answer is simple: that person doesn't have a personal relationship with God. When someone has a true relationship with God, it doesn't matter what message the outside world conveys. The message God has for that person will be given by Him. It may come directly or indirectly but the person will know because of his or her relationship with God. He or she will be convinced in heart and spirit, and the actions will flow through the person's body.

Generally, people establish a relationship with God through religion. Whether someone is Christian, Jewish, Islamic, Muslim, Hindu, Buddhist, etc., people strengthen their relationship with God when they abide by a set of practices and customs established by a religion. Often we find a relationship with God via practicing pre-established patterns or customs. Religion is often practiced and experienced in community, which has numerous benefits; for example, it prevents us from feeling alone in the struggles of daily life. I grew up Christian so my references will be based on Christian practices and customs.

God = Love

I'd like to make a distinction between religion and spirituality, which is our personal relationship with God. **Religion tells us that God's love is conditional, whereas spirituality tells us that God's love is unconditional.** I view spirituality as intimate, which means that initially it can only be experienced between an individual and God. (I say *initially* because, in my opinion, you can eventually also be spiritually connected to your life partner or spouse, the person God has ordained for you.) It's through this intimate relationship with God Himself that our mind and spirit are allowed to realize that God is love; there is nothing we can do or not do to separate ourselves from His love.

Addiction equals pain—we've established that. And our fear motivates us to put up walls that prevent us from getting to the source(s) of pain. I say, it's time to tear down those walls. I sincerely hope that you are willing to accompany me on a

Introduction

journey to discover how we can use the 4 STEPS to break the addictive cycle and get to the root of our pain. Although I am not a therapist or licensed professional counselor like my mother, I know what it feels like to struggle with an addiction. I repeated the addictive cycle for years, and I wasn't able to truly break out of it until I established and intentionally utilized the 4 STEPS. I'm not going to lie and tell you it will be easy. But I can promise you that it will be worth it—because you are worthy of love. Unconditional love and acceptance from yourself, others and the Source of Love is available to you just as you are, no matter what you've been told in the past. The key is to address the pain. **What we don't address, we can't change.**

This workbook is specifically designed so that you can write your thoughts and feelings on these pages; I hope you'll use it as you would a journal.

Helping Others in the Journey,

A.D. Burks

STEP 1

Re/Establish Your Relationship with God

The prodigal son, I had become;
Deliberately and defiantly veering off course.
Yet patiently You called me
Then I finally sought the One.
—*The Answer, A.D. Burks*
From *Sex and Surrender: An Addict's Journey*

Re/Establish Your Relationship with God

STEP 1 is the most important step in the 4 STEPS. Without STEP 1, the remaining three steps are useless. And it makes no sense to skip STEP 1 and go to the other steps because it won't work. The 4 STEPS are cumulative, and STEP 1 is the foundation: you establish your own relationship with God. Once that foundation is in place, you have established the momentum to break the addictive cycle. A personal relationship with God will help guide and support you through the remaining steps. (I used the "/" in the title— "Re/Establish Your Relationship with God'—because although some of you may have already established your own relationship with God, you might have allowed the relationship to slip from being the number-one priority in your life.)

Because addictions feed the ego, they are by their very nature self-indulgent. Not only does the addiction hurt the addict, it also creates collateral damage in the lives of the addict's friends and family members. The addiction takes control of the addict's mind and he or she is unable to logically process the damage to self and/or others. Addicts begin to view themselves and their pain as the center of the world; the best way to counter this belief is to connect with and establish a personal relationship with the Source of Life/Source of Love/God.

Trust and Commitment

Two requirements for any "real" relationship are trust and commitment. Often, though, in relationships with friends, family or co-workers, we either don't trust or we can't commit. You can trust someone but that doesn't mean you're committed to doing what's best for that person and vice versa. Or you can be committed to a person, but you may not trust him or her. For example, you might have heard someone say, "I love him, but I don't trust him." Parents can love their children unconditionally, but that doesn't mean they always trust their children to do what they promise or say. Similarly, a child can love a parent unconditionally, but that doesn't mean she can trust that parent to provide emotional support, especially when the parent is unavailable or preoccupied.

We tend to approach trust in two ways: either I trust you until you prove you can't be trusted, or I'll trust you when you prove you are trustworthy. The differing approaches are typically influenced by a person's upbringing. If a child is raised in an environment in which he was able to trust those around him, he will be more inclined initially to trust a person. But if a child was raised in an environment in which promises were consistently broken and trust was an issue, she may be unable initially to trust. The same goes for our relationship with God. If a person can't have a real relationship with God, how can you expect him or her to have a real relationship with you?

Commitment can be in place even when there is no trust. I've had jobs in which I was committed to showing up day after day to complete the tasks listed in my job description, but I didn't trust my supervisor. In one particular instance, that trust was broken when a supervisor told me that I had received the promotion he recommended me for, when in fact that was not the case. My job title and pay did not change, but my workload definitely increased. I was still committed to coming to work and doing my job because I needed the income, but I wasn't naïve enough to trust this particular supervisor again.

Commitment isn't always convenient. In the work situation I described above, if my supervisor had been committed to his word, he would have found a way to follow through with his commitment even if his supervisor had informed him that the job structure had changed. Instead, he chose to lie by equivocating about what he had originally said.

Thankfully, God doesn't lie. When He makes a promise He keeps it. Too often, though, we don't follow through on the promises we make to Him. Often we make a pact with God, promising Him that if we get what we want, we'll either forgo a behavior or change it. After the commitment has been established, God does come through as He always does, but we get so elated or relieved when the stressful situation is resolved that we conveniently forget to follow through on our part of the commitment. So what happens?

God demonstrates that He was committed to doing what He said and proves that we can trust Him, but we don't prove to Him that we can be trusted because we don't uphold our part of the commitment. Despite our lack of commitment, God still loves us. Some people believe that when a person fails to follow through on a commitment even once, he or she is no longer worthy of trust. And if someone consistently breaks promises there is no way they'll ever trust him or her. Thankfully, God is not a man and His grace and mercy allows Him to continue to love us regardless of our occasional lack of commitment. When it becomes difficult to follow through with a commitment, it makes sense to focus on the reason why you made the commitment in the first place.

Sin

Yes, that three-letter word that we all want to point out to someone else but can't bear to have it pointed out to us. Like most things in life, definitions and interpretations of what constitutes "sin" vary. Pastors, churchgoers and even non-religious people will tell you what is and is not a sin. Their definition is typically based on scripture, or on their interpretation or someone else's interpretation of scripture.

The best definition that I've heard for sin is *anything that separates one from God*. I love that definition because it eliminates what I call the bait and switch method—our urge to debate which sin(s) are worse than others. It's easy to focus on one particular "sin" and then condemn anyone who engages in it or struggles with it. Focusing on others' sins is a convenient way to avoid looking at your own. Scripture says, *for all have sinned and fall short of the glory of God (Romans 3:23).*

I don't quote scripture here in order to point a finger at those who use scripture to vilify others; instead, I want to show how easy it is to take scripture out of context to "prove" one ideology right and another wrong. In fact, Romans 3:23 says that no sin is worse than another and that no one has a warrant on God's love. God is about love and forgiveness, not separation and damnation. The true foundation of Christianity is based on the belief that God sent Jesus as the sacrificial lamb to bring all of us back into relationship with Him.

Let's avoid the tendency to focus on the sin versus the Savior. If we intentionally focus our attention on the Savior, it's easier to see God's love for all. *For I am convinced that neither death nor life, neither angels nor demons, neither the present nor the future, nor any powers, neither height nor depth, nor anything else in all creation, will be able to separate us from the love of God that is in Christ Jesus our Lord (Romans 8:38-39)*. It's simple: nothing can separate us from God's love.

So why do addicts feel they can't have a personal relationship with God? Could it be because they are relying on someone else to establish that relationship for them? You get what you give. Or, as one of my finance professors used to say, "There is no free lunch." These days we're very aware of the disease of entitlement. If you're financially well off, it might be easy to rationalize that you deserve privilege or that you somehow earned it, but that doesn't transfer to the spiritual world. On the spiritual plane, everyone is equal. It doesn't matter how much you have or don't have; God sees, treats and loves us all the same.

STEP 1

Pain

If God loves us all and sin can't separate us, why do we experience pain? It simply isn't true that once we realize that God loves us unconditionally we can do whatever we want and there will be no repercussions. That is not the reality.

Realistically, if we all did whatever we wanted we'd be living in a world of chaos and extinction. It is a law of nature that everything has an equal and opposite reaction, and that still holds true despite God's unconditional love. We will indeed experience repercussions for our actions, and sometimes that repercussion is pain.

We also experience pain to let us know when we fail to keep God's will for our life. He has a purpose for us being on earth, and when we get off course, we often experience pain—this is God's way of trying to get us back on the right path. For instance, I grew up singing in the church choir from the age of four. I went on to place in the University Interscholastic League Texas State Solo & Ensemble performance when I was in middle school. In college I had the opportunity to sing at Carnegie Hall with the Grinnell Singers. I even went to Atlanta to pursue a music career and trained and traveled internationally with a singing coach who worked with several LaFace & Arista recording artists.

Singing and music was and always will be one of my passions, but despite the time, energy and money I spent trying to become a professional singer, it never happened. Why? Because God wanted me to do what I'm doing right now: using my gift of writing to let people know that God loves them just as they are and that they can form their own relationship with Him no matter what they've been told or believed in the past.

This might be the next logical question that arises: if God knew you weren't going to become a professional singer, why would He allow you to put in all that work for nothing? Thankfully, I can tell you it wasn't for nothing. That work became a testament to the lessons I learned in the process. And the work ended up strengthening my relationship with God when it felt like the floor was falling out from under me.

God never leaves you, but he does at times allow pain to correct you.

Happiness vs. Joy

Once you establish a relationship with God, or once you give your life to Christ, everything will not be perfect; to believe so would be delusional. While most people feel immense joy the moment they establish or re-establish their relationship with God, that joy is not the same as happiness.

STEP 1

Happiness is situational, while joy is eternal. Put another way, happiness can be taken away, but nothing can steal a person's joy. The foundation of joy is built on a personal relationship with God. Experiencing happiness is easy, but understanding and maintaining joy requires work. And that work is simply to establish and build a personal relationship with God, so you know His will for your life.

When things go the way I want, I'm usually happy. Let's say I purchase tickets for a concert and I'm able to get the last seats available, a situation that actually happened this week. I was extremely happy. But if the same situation had gone down in a different way and I wasn't able to get those tickets, I wouldn't have been happy at all. In fact, I would have been pissed because I really wanted to go to the event. Clearly, my happiness is based on the outcome of the situation going in my favor.

Joy is different, though—it is not dependent on things going my way. When I was pursuing a music career and things didn't work out the way I had planned I wasn't happy at all. As a matter of fact, I was so distraught that I felt lost and hopeless. I had done everything to ensure that I would become a professional singer and songwriter, but it didn't happen.

The 4 STEPS

So how did I deal with the pain? I subconsciously turned to my addiction. It's so easy to run to whatever things we addicts believe we can control to deal with the pain. But in reality the addiction is preventing us from tapping into and experiencing joy.

Joy says, even though things aren't going my way, I know God is using this particular situation or event to help prepare me for my purpose. Joy says, even though it feels like my world is falling apart right before my eyes, I know this too shall pass. Joy says, after I've given my very best and things still aren't happening as I think they should (I'm not getting the love I need from my partner, my health isn't improving like the doctors said it would), God will use all of it for my good and the purpose He has placed me on this earth to fulfill.

To experience that level of joy, a person not only has to have a relationship with God, but a relationship in which trust and commitment have been tested. It is in the testing of that relationship that God proves He can be trusted, because He's committed to doing what's best for you.

When the real estate market went through one of its downturns in 2005, I was informed by my division president that I was going to be downsized. Of course, no one wants to hear that they are about to be fired, but I felt blessed to have been informed ahead of time so I could start looking. I could see that God had already made preparations.

I updated my resume and called the people in my extensive network to inform them that I was looking for a job. I didn't let pride or ego stifle me. It's a given that whenever you work for someone else you can be fired; I accepted that and didn't let ego and pride prevent me from receiving God's next blessing.

The entire real estate market was plummeting at this time, so most of my contacts didn't know of any opportunities. Within a few weeks, though, I got a call from a childhood friend asking if I was looking for a job. She told me about a position at the oil and gas company where she worked and she sent me the job description.

It turned out that the skill set for this particular position was very specific, and there were no qualified internal candidates. There's a saying: what God has for you, is for you.

At this time, I was also in the process of obtaining a construction loan to build my first duplex. I was very worried about how I was going to continue with the construction, since I wasn't sure I would have income (thankfully, I did have savings). Then I got a call saying that I had an interview at the new company. I knew at that moment that God was telling me, don't worry, I have everything under control.

God worked it out so that I got the job, had three weeks off before I started, was approved for the construction loan, and got a $20,000 pay raise.

I'm not telling that story to brag about how good God has been to me. I mean to show that when I was at one of the lowest points in my life and had no idea where my next dollar was coming from, God already had everything set up and under control. That's why it's so important to have a relationship with God and know you aren't working for some company; you're working for Him. When we trust and commit our lives to Him, we open ourselves to experience not just happiness but joy. Because God has a purpose for our lives!

Living with a Purpose

When was the last time you asked, what is my purpose? I'll never forget the summer after I graduated from Grinnell College. Although I had a chemistry degree, I didn't want to be a chemist, I no longer wanted to go to medical school, and pursuing a professional singing career wasn't proceeding the way I had hoped. That summer I took on some odd jobs to make money, but nothing that made me feel like I was living with a purpose.

It was such a lonely and bewildering period. All my college friends were in different cities and states and some were going to graduate school or starting their respective careers. Time away from all the noise and influence of others creates a space for personal reflection, and that can be quite uncomfortable if it isn't one's normal mode of operation. Now that I had time to reflect, I started to ask: why had I been put on this earth? What am I good at? What have others told me I'm good at? What do I enjoy doing? Besides external validation, I wanted to wake up each morning excited about the rest of my life.

No matter how much energy I put into researching, contemplating and talking with others, I never came to an answer that felt good inside. So after I had looked everywhere but to God, I decided I'd try hearing what God had to say. I wondered if perhaps doing something I'd never done before might be the answer. I'd always heard in church that if you wanted an answer from God you had to fast and pray. Praying wasn't an issue, but fasting wasn't on my typical to-do list. But I needed an answer.

I decided I would abstain from food but would drink water. Since I was young, in my early twenties, naïve, and impatient, that fast didn't last. I fasted and prayed for an entire day, but I still didn't get an answer, much less the one I was looking for. I'm sure people who practice fasting would tell me you have to do it for more than a day. I had to be honest with myself, that wasn't my thing. And I knew that God meets each of us right where we are. When I reflect on this time, I realize that it just wasn't my time yet to know or understand my purpose.

This goes to a crucial point:

Just because you haven't found your purpose doesn't mean you should stop searching or turn towards an addiction to deal with the pain. It would be over twelve years before I understood what my purpose was. Before I could get to the place of understanding my purpose, I had to endure my attempts at being a professional singer, had to earn my MBA, and I had to experience addiction.

If I had known the extent of the pain I would endure or the amount of work required, I never would have done it. And that goes to my second point: *God doesn't always reveal His purpose or plan for your life when you want Him to because you might not be able or ready to handle it at the time.* This is when trust, faith, commitment and obedience come into play. I had to trust that God still loved me and would take care of me even though I had no idea why I was living through pain and loss.

And here's yet another point: *God's plan(s) and purpose(s) for your life will often defy logic.* If your purpose in life could be achieved and understood via logic alone, it would be so easy to dismiss God's role. If logic was all that was required, you wouldn't have to establish your own relationship with God. When you can't logically explain things, when you realize that your own wisdom or power can't explain how you achieved a certain goal or outcome, or when you survived when you could have just as easily died, that is when you really know for yourself that God loves you and is committed to you. You can trust God, and so it's easy to be obedient to what He's telling you to do because you've seen the benefits for yourself.

How do I know? I know because I've been through the pain and I've come out the other side. I can look back and see how God's love kept me when I should have been dead. I have achieved things for which there is no logical explanation. And more importantly, I'm being obedient at this moment by writing about my experiences; I hope my words will serve to inspire you to establish or re-establish your own relationship with God because you deserve to live your life with purpose.

Forgiveness

When I was in the process of writing this book, I asked a friend, a former addict who went through the 12 Steps, to read it. He was very encouraging and mentioned I might want to add some material about forgiveness. I'm so grateful that he did. As the grandson of a Baptist preacher, I take for granted the ability to forgive myself and others because it is such a part of my family culture. Even now I can hear my mom saying, "If I make a mistake, all I can do is ask for your forgiveness." She would not only ask for another person's forgiveness, but she too was always willing to forgive others and not to hold a grudge.

When I was a child, I was sick and had to take a liquid medicine with the worse taste in the world. I couldn't even get it down. My mom knew I needed to take the medicine to get better, so when I refused to take it she gave me a whipping. I cried and cried, and then I told her, "You take it!" So she did and immediately said, "I'm sorry, you're right." Then she called the doctor and had him prescribe another medication in pill form.

That example illustrates an important reality: how we see the world as adults is based on childhood experiences (or the fact that we missed out on certain experiences). My mother was able to be vulnerable, to admit that she was wrong, and to ask for my forgiveness, and that helps me realize that we all make mistakes, even the people who love us the most. The key is being humble enough to admit the mistake and to sincerely ask for forgiveness.

If I had grown up in a household in which my parents were

STEP 1

unable to forgive or ask for forgiveness, I would be less likely to forgive myself and others, an essential attribute. If we aren't able to forgive ourselves, why would we be able to forgive others? After all, how can I give you what I don't have?

Christianity is based on the belief that God sent Jesus to serve as the sacrificial lamb for the forgiveness of the sins of all humanity. So whatever mistake you have made or sin committed, God has already granted you forgiveness through Christ. Unless you can accept that you've been forgiven, you won't be able to forgive yourself, much less anyone else.

There is no mistake that renders us unforgivable. For me, the reality is that my relationship with God has confirmed my capacity to be forgiven and to forgive. That doesn't mean I should keep making the same mistake, but it does mean that I can forgive myself and make a concerted effort not to repeat my mistakes. And if I can extend that forgiveness to myself, I also have to extend it to others. When I choose not to forgive another person's mistake, it doesn't hurt that person; ultimately, it hurts me

STEP 1 QUESTIONS

At this juncture I hope you are thinking about ways to establish or re-establish your relationship with God. To have a relationship with the God of your understanding you do not have to claim, commit to or affiliate with any particular religion or religious sect. Below are some prompts to help you think through the questions and/or write answers to them. Thinking about a question is good, but physically writing something out requires a deeper level of thought and understanding. It also serves as a visual reminder of where you were at a particular point in life. Being able to look back and see where I was in life and how God helped me grow strengthens my relationship with Him. These questions aren't meant to be answered in one sitting, so please allot enough time to create thorough responses. If you need to come back to them, please do so, but don't rush the process. Taking the time to go through the process allows you to make a breakthrough and move toward the relationship you desire.

The 4 STEPS

TRUST AND COMMITMENT

What commitments have you made in the past with God when He delivered on His end but you didn't?

_____

_____

_____

_____

_____

_____

_____

_____

_____

_____

_____

_____

_____

_____

_____

STEP 1 Questions

Have you still been able to go to God even when you didn't follow through on that commitment? If so, how does that make you feel? Unconditionally loved? Blessed? Have you taken His love for granted?

_____

_____

_____

_____

_____

_____

_____

_____

_____

_____

_____

_____

_____

The 4 STEPS

If you haven't been able to go back to God, why not?

STEP 1 Questions

What has God done to prove you can trust Him?

The 4 STEPS

What have you done to prove to God He can trust you?

_____
_____
_____
_____
_____
_____
_____
_____
_____
_____
_____
_____
_____
_____
_____

SIN

Do you feel you don't deserve to be loved by God because of something you have done or have failed to do? Do you feel guilty and what is the source of the guilt?

_____

_____

_____

_____

_____

_____

_____

_____

_____

_____

_____

_____

_____

_____

The 4 STEPS

Have you been told or read somewhere that God won't forgive you? Do you believe God won't forgive you? Why?

STEP 1 Questions

What kind of relationship is that? Is it a spiritual relationship?

The 4 STEPS

Are your beliefs about what you consider to be a sin based on what someone has told you or on what God has told you?

_____

_____

_____

_____

_____

_____

_____

_____

_____

_____

_____

_____

_____

_____

_____

_____

STEP 1 Questions

Have you asked God for discernment on what you have read regarding sin? Are you aware of the context, meaning, and origin of that particular text?

The 4 STEPS

PAIN

What is the most painful thing you have experienced?

___

STEP 1 Questions

Be honest with yourself: have you really gotten over it?

The 4 STEPS

If you have gone through it, how or what did you do to get through it? If you haven't, what are you doing or not doing to cope?

_____

_____

_____

_____

_____

_____

_____

_____

_____

_____

_____

_____

_____

_____

_____

_____

STEP 1 Questions

Do you feel your addiction has reached a point at which there is nothing you or God can do to break the cycle? If so, why? (The fact that you are alive means you have another opportunity to get it right!)

_____

_____

_____

_____

_____

_____

_____

_____

_____

_____

_____

_____

_____

_____

_____

HAPPINESS VS. JOY

How do you define happiness versus joy?

STEP 1 Questions

What is the happiest moment in your life? Who was there and where are they now?

_____

_____

_____

_____

_____

_____

_____

_____

_____

_____

_____

_____

_____

_____

_____

_____

The 4 STEPS

Have you ever felt joy (calmness or a sense of peace) in the middle of a difficult situation(s)?

___
___
___
___
___
___
___
___
___
___
___
___
___
___
___

STEP 1 Questions

If so, what did that joy feel like? What and where were you during that moment(s) of peace?

_____
_____
_____
_____
_____
_____
_____
_____
_____
_____
_____
_____
_____
_____
_____
_____

The 4 STEPS

LIVING WITH A PURPOSE

What are some things God has done for you that you or anyone else couldn't do for yourself?

_____

_____

_____

_____

_____

_____

_____

_____

_____

_____

_____

_____

_____

_____

STEP 1 Questions

Where do you experience God?

The 4 STEPS

When do you experience God?

STEP 1 Questions

What do you do to strengthen your relationship with God?

The 4 STEPS

Have you found your God-given purpose(s)? What is it?

_____

_____

_____

_____

_____

_____

_____

_____

_____

_____

_____

_____

_____

_____

_____

_____

STEP 1 Questions

If you haven't found your purpose, are you pursuing positive things that you are passionate about?

The 4 STEPS

What gifts, talents or abilities do people who love you unconditionally say you possess?

___

___

___

___

___

___

___

___

___

___

___

___

___

___

___

STEP 1 Questions

What are you doing on a daily basis to fulfill and/or pursue your God-given purpose?

FORGIVENESS

Which of your mistake(s) do you believe are too great for God to forgive? Why?

_____

_____

_____

_____

_____

_____

_____

_____

_____

_____

_____

_____

_____

_____

_____

STEP 1 Questions

What mistakes have you not forgiven yourself for? Why?

The 4 STEPS

Who haven't you forgiven? Why?

STEP 1 Questions

What would happen if you chose to forgive him or her?

_____
_____
_____
_____
_____
_____
_____
_____
_____
_____
_____
_____
_____
_____
_____
_____

The 4 STEPS

Whom do you need to ask forgiveness of? What has stopped you from asking?

_____

_____

_____

_____

_____

_____

_____

_____

_____

_____

_____

_____

_____

_____

_____

_____

_____

_____

STEP 2

Abstinence

> *While being enraptured by lust,*
> *Never allow yourself to be naïve and trust*
> *The thought "it's okay."*
> *Today might very well be the day.*
> *—Unprotected, A.D. Burks*
> From *Sex and Surrender: An Addict's Journey*

Abstinence

Now that you have taken the most important step of establishing or re-establishing your relationship with God, you are ready for the next step. This does not mean that the work you did in STEP 1 is finished. Just as with any intimate relationship, you have to work at it daily, but the rewards are worth all the effort. The work you completed in STEP 1 has prepared you and will sustain you through STEP 2, especially when things get tough and you want to give up. Always remember that God loves you and that He's going to support you during this period of abstinence. One way to view this period is as an opportunity to remove the very thing that is preventing you from getting closer to God/Love.

No matter what your addiction—alcohol, sex, drugs, food, gambling, etc.—at some point, you will have to abstain from it if you are going to break the addictive cycle. When it comes to substances or behaviors that are not essential for you to live (e.g., non-prescription drugs, smoking, gambling) I would suggest you curtail them completely and never go back.

Of course, certain addictions are part of everyday life and cannot be eliminated entirely (e.g., food, prescription drugs, and sex, which are necessary for one's overall health). Instituting a period of abstinence from those particular addictions will be different.

Food, Prescription Drugs, and Sex

We all need to eat in order to survive, but we need to be careful about our food choices. For those who are addicted to food, such items as cake, pie, potato chips, fried food and other processed items can be triggers. During my early adolescence I was a chubby and overweight kid. Although I didn't have an actual food addiction, I know what it is like to struggle with food.

My parents divorced when I was four, and that was extremely painful for the entire family. Since my mom had primary custody of me, I was indirectly more privy to her pain than to my father's. Because she was an astute, licensed professional counselor, she did everything in her power to make sure I had the best childhood possible, but she was finding ways to deal with her pain: she turned to food—specifically, to sweets and sugar. Her preferred drug of choice was vanilla ice cream. After we had a very nutritionally balanced meal, which she carefully prepared, we would have a very generous bowl (not cup) of Blue Bell vanilla ice cream. Notice I said "we."

Sugar is one of the most addictive legal drugs in America. The nation's obesity rate continues to skyrocket, thanks in large part to the ample access we have to sugar in countless forms: from the obvious candy, cake, and pastries to the more hidden sources, like ketchup, salad dressings and lattes.

As a child, I wasn't aware that high sugar intake was the reason I was overweight. And as an adult, I don't vilify my mom for raising an obese child. She provided a stable educational, spiritual, and emotional environment, and she protected me from her own pain in the best way she knew. Today I take personal responsibility and I recognize that I am susceptible to using sugar to deal with pain, and for that reason I am vigilant about occasions when I might turn to sweets.

I'm thankful that my propensity for sugar didn't turn into a food addiction and that when I reached high school I was able to lose the excess weight. But I am acutely aware that I could have just as easily ended up dealing with diabetes and hypertension. We all know that purchasing processed food is substantially cheaper than buying healthy fruits and vegetables, and this makes lower-income people particularly vulnerable. It is important to abstain from high glycemic and processed food so our bodies have a chance to function properly. I know that this is easier said than done, but there are programs that will provide support. Seek and ye shall find!

Let's focus for a moment on the challenge of prescription drugs. It is widely known that overmedicating on prescription drugs, such as painkillers, can easily turn into an addiction. And this can sometimes be insidious in that we expect street drugs or recreational drugs, such as cocaine or heroin, to be off-limits when we talk about abstinence, but prescription drugs can be a slippery slope. If you have been prescribed medication by a physician, then your challenge is to take that medication in the prescribed dosage only.

Some of my family members are on daily pain medication, and so I have true compassion and empathy for people who must take such medication. For some, physical pain is 24/7, but others may be over-medicating to escape psychological pain. Even though the effect of the painkillers wears off, the psychological and emotional pain remains. I ask you to reflect and to seek a situation of balanced psychological health.

Let's also think about abstinence with regard to sex: abstinence is not the same as celibacy. Several scientific studies confirm the benefits of sex and a healthy sex life. As a former sex addict, abstaining from sex was paramount for me to break the addictive cycle. Abstinence allowed me to understand how sex was affecting me and how to place sex in its intended place in my life. Sex is a wonderful spiritual experience, but if we use it to escape pain, it becomes addictive. And that means that we need to choose a period of abstinence in order to break the addictive nature of sex. Once an addict is able to understand why he or she is using sex to escape pain and implement coping mechanisms to break that pattern, he or she will be able to reengage in sex in a way that will benefit both self and partner.

Forced, Self-Imposed or Chosen

The mindset you take towards abstinence determines the results. I abstained from sex for three different periods in my life and each time I got a different result. Now that I have broken the addictive cycle and understand the root causes of my pain, I am able to discern how my reasoning for abstaining from sex at different points in my life resulted in different outcomes.

The first time I practiced abstinence I felt forced. The next time it was self-imposed and the last instance was a personal choice. Why am I taking the time to differentiate these results?

When I felt forced and when I imposed a period of abstinence on myself, I found myself back in the addictive cycle. As a point of clarification, I want to emphasize that I *felt* forced. We tend to think that being "forced" means being physically restrained or legally ordered, but what I mean here is that feeling shame and trying to please people, especially the ones you love, can make you *feel* forced. That was not where I wanted to be, nor is it where I want someone who's working STEP 2 to be. It was only when I *chose* abstinence for myself, not out of fear, or in an attempt to please someone else, that I was finally able to get the intended benefit of not using my addiction to escape pain.

After I received my undergraduate degree in chemistry, I wanted to pursue music full-time. My mother's brother knew a former record producer in Nashville, and the majority of my father's family lived in the city. Nashville was the country music capital of the world, and although country was not my preferred genre, I decided to move there, to just take a risk and see what might happen. I had some experience in concert promotion, so I planned to work with my older cousin, who was a businessman looking to get into concert promotions.

I was in the early stages of my addiction. Although I didn't know it, I was putting to the test two of the root causes of my sex addiction: refusing to accept my sexuality and trying to please the people I love. I looked up to my cousin because he was the closest person I had to a brother, and I wanted to please him. As soon as I got to the city, I was labeled as his intelligent and attractive cousin from Texas, and was viewed as one of the boys. My cousin had a reputation as a playboy, and so in order to keep up appearances I felt forced to hide my sexuality and practice abstinence. While I wasn't literally forced to hide my sexuality, I felt immense pressure to do so because of the way homosexuality was regarded in our family, community and spiritual upbringing.

Being in a situation where I felt forced to practice abstinence defeated the purpose. I was focused on hiding and people pleasing instead of focusing on the reasons for and benefits of abstinence. If an addict is forced to abstain from his addiction because of a court mandate or in an attempt to please others, he may end up returning to the addictive cycle.

Feeling as if you're forced into abstinence is definitely not the intent for implementing STEP 2, and neither is self-imposed abstinence. After Nashville, I moved to Atlanta to continue my music career. It was the first time I had moved to a place where I didn't have blood relatives and well-established friendships, and it was the time when I felt the most alone in my life. Being alone was painful, for sure, but one of the positive unanticipated benefits is that I was able to clearly hear God speaking to me.

Often addicts turn to their addiction to escape pain. For an extrovert like me, feeling lonely can be worse than physical pain. But in this particular instance I was determined not to turn to sex. Subconsciously, I was probably afraid that if I engaged in anonymous sex in a city where I didn't really know anyone and didn't have a well-established support system I might find myself in a situation I wouldn't be able to get out of. Also, I had just come from Nashville, where I felt forced to stop acting out sexually, so my urge wasn't as strong as it had been in the early days of my addiction. Humans are creatures of habit and our brains will react in the way we train them to. The biggest reason, though, was that I thought if I abstained from "sinful sex" God would give me the music career I had been dreaming about.

Basically, I was imposing abstinence on myself in an effort to get something from God. **You can't manipulate God the way you manipulate your addiction.** Or, I should say, the way you *think* you're manipulating your addiction, since we are often kidding ourselves about being in control. God doesn't operate the way we humans do—that is, on the barter system. *If you do this for me, God, I'll do that for you.* God wants what's best for you and that means you don't necessarily get to

STEP 2

have what you think you want or need. When I look back, I realize that if God had given me the music career I so desperately wanted and worked for, I would have gone deeper into my addictive cycle because sex would have been more accessible. With money, fame and power comes more opportunities to abuse substances and people, which is why celebrities end up in rehab, often more than once. Until a person has a personal relationship with God and is obedient to what He is telling him or her, I don't believe an addictive cycle can truly be broken. The next step in that process is choosing abstinence.

Life is filled with choices. Some of the choices I've made in my life were very strategic and led me to some amazing opportunities. Conversely, I made some choices that led to epic failures. Those collective choices have made me the person I am and led me to where I am right now: I am no longer struggling and using sex to escape pain. Here's what made the difference: I made the decision to abstain from sex instead of being forced, coerced, cajoled or shamed into abstinence. By taking personal accountability for my actions, I gained a deeper understanding of why abstaining from sex was so important in breaking the addictive cycle. No one, not even God, could make the choice for me. We are given free will and when we choose to exercise it for our benefit, the possibilities are endless.

The Challenge

What led me to choose abstinence of my own free will? A challenge! A fellow writer and friend saw my destructive relationship/sex addictive cycle. When we were at my house one day, I was just coming out of a very unhealthy relationship and he suggested I take a break from relationships and sex for nine months.

When I was in Atlanta I was abstinent for a year and a half, but not because I chose to be—I was motivated by fear. So I knew I could do nine months. It wouldn't be easy but I could do it. So at that moment I decided I would abstain from sex for nine months and also refrain from getting into a serious relationship.

It was one of the best decisions I ever made. By choosing not to have sex or get serious with anyone, I was able to see clearly the true reason I was interacting with people. Once sex was no longer an option, certain people were no longer an option. I stopped wasting time plotting, scheming and manipulating in order to become intimate with others, and instead I was finally able to look at myself.

I cleared my mind of unhealthy thoughts regarding sex, and that allowed me to see that sex is a spiritual act; I now understood that I should only engage in sex with someone with whom I had a spiritual connection. In the past, when I had suffered over not having the family I wanted, I would turn to sex to escape the pain, but now I was forced to really deal with the pain. *Trying to avoid the pain doesn't make it go away!*

Making a Decision

For nine months I sat in the pain with my therapist and we worked through it together. What was truly ironic is that after nine months, I still didn't have sex. More than a year went by before I had sex again. I had made the decision that I wasn't going to have sex unless there was a spiritual connection between myself and another person. It was great to let someone I was dating know up front that sex wasn't an option unless and until there was a spiritual connection. Initially, that reality scared a few people away, and that was my intention. Many people don't understand the true meaning of sex and I didn't need or want to be in a relationship with those people. Others decided to see if I was serious by trying to tempt and test me. It was challenging at times. In the past, beautiful faces and bodies were justification for having sex. But this was a new day and I had a new awareness of why and how I would engage in sex. So when the test came, I passed.

The 4 STEPS

At one point, I began dating an extremely attractive person; in the past, I would have had sex with him in the first week, if not the first night. But I let it be known from the start that I was looking for someone I could marry and have a family with. This person talked about having children and other similar goals. After a while, though, I realized he wanted a family, but not until later in life—right now, he was only looking for sex. Here's what I believe: God/the Universe won't allow a person into the Promised Land until he or she passes the test—that is, the test of whether the person with whom you're having sex is the one God has ordained for you. Another way to say this: ask yourself if you feel a genuine spiritual connection with this person. In this instance, although I really wanted to have sex, I decided against it because I didn't really have a spiritual connection with this person. Ultimately, passing that test opened a path for the person I did have a spiritual connection with to come into my life, someone who was serious about having a family in the present. I am so grateful for this gift.

The formation of the IT'S OK 2W8 (It's Okay to Wait) Campaign (www.itsok2w8.com) was another benefit of my period of abstinence. Although I didn't start the campaign until a few years after my period of abstinence, I never would have initiated it if I had not chosen to be abstinent.

The focus of the campaign is encouraging people to commit

to waiting to have sex until they know their own and their partners' HIV and STD status. I figured that if I could help people focus on their sexual health, I could help reduce the spread of sexually transmitted diseases.

(In 2014, the Centers for Disease Control and Prevention reported that the highest HIV infection rates were among people who were between the ages of 13 and 24.)

STEP 2 QUESTIONS

If you asked me if I would do it all again, I would immediately say yes. Choosing abstinence not only allowed me to hear God's voice more clearly, it also allowed me to trust God more. I chose to step away from the addictive cycle and deal directly with the sources of the pain rather than avoid them. I was able to lay the foundation to pass the test of temptation, and that allowed me to step onto the path of the life I truly wanted.

It is my hope that you have been inspired by my journey and are now asking some of the following questions: What will allow me to engage in a period of abstinence? Am I strong enough? What happens when I get tempted? What if I relapse? Is it really worth it?

If I did it, and so can you!! One verse has always stayed in my mind: *I can do all things through Christ who strengthens me (Philippians 4:13)*. Of course, you don't need to be a Christian to begin this journey; ideally, you have already worked STEP 1 and have established or re-established your relationship with the divine source or higher power. And you are secure in the knowledge that you don't have to rely on your own strength to get through STEP 2 alone.

Here are some questions to consider as you work STEP 2:

The 4 STEPS

ABSTINENCE

What addiction(s) do you need to abstain from and never return to? Is it drugs, alcohol, smoking, self-mutilation, etc.?

_____

_____

_____

_____

_____

_____

_____

_____

_____

_____

_____

_____

_____

_____

_____

STEP 2 Questions

If you ended up reengaging in the addiction after a period of abstinence, what would you gain?

_____

_____

_____

_____

_____

_____

_____

_____

_____

_____

_____

_____

_____

_____

_____

_____

The 4 STEPS

What would you lose?

STEP 2 Questions

FOOD, PRESCRIPTION DRUGS, SEX, AND OTHER ADDICTIONS

Is your addictive substance something you must learn to use in a healthy manner? For example, food, prescription drugs, sex, or exercise. How can you plan to abstain for a specific period? How can you safely return?

The 4 STEPS

What would it look like for you to have a healthy relationship with this particular substance or behavior?

_____

_____

_____

_____

_____

_____

_____

_____

_____

_____

_____

_____

_____

_____

_____

STEP 2 Questions

Are there resources or professionals who can help you determine what healthy looks like for this particular substance(s) or behavior(s)?

_____

_____

_____

_____

_____

_____

_____

_____

_____

_____

_____

_____

_____

_____

The 4 STEPS

What benefits would you gain by engaging in the substance(s) or behavior(s) in a healthy manner?

_____

_____

_____

_____

_____

_____

_____

_____

_____

_____

_____

_____

_____

_____

_____

_____

STEP 2 Questions

What would you lose by engaging in the substance(s) or behavior(s) in a healthy manner?

The 4 STEPS

FORCED, SELF-IMPOSED OR CHOSEN

Have you ever been forced to abstain from your addiction(s)? Who mandated the period of abstinence?

STEP 2 Questions

How did being forced make you feel?

The 4 STEPS

How did you feel during that period of abstinence?

_____
_____
_____
_____
_____
_____
_____
_____
_____
_____
_____
_____
_____
_____
_____
_____
_____
_____
_____

Did you learn anything detrimental or beneficial during that period of abstinence?

The 4 STEPS

Are you resentful towards a person or a group of people for being forced into a period of abstinence against your own free will? Who is it or who are they? If so, what is preventing you from forgiving that person(s)? Is there a way for you to visualize being free of the resentment?

_____
_____
_____
_____
_____
_____
_____
_____
_____
_____
_____
_____
_____
_____
_____

STEP 2 Questions

Have you ever imposed a period of abstinence on yourself? If so, what motivated you?

The 4 STEPS

Did you learn anything detrimental or beneficial during that period of self-imposed abstinence?

STEP 2 Questions

Do you hold any resentment towards yourself for imposing a period of abstinence? If so, why and what are you gaining or losing by not letting it go?

_____

_____

_____

_____

_____

_____

_____

_____

_____

_____

_____

_____

_____

_____

The 4 STEPS

What is your biggest fear about abstaining from your addiction? (Describe in detail what this fear/situation looks like to you.)

_____

_____

_____

_____

_____

_____

_____

_____

_____

_____

_____

_____

_____

_____

_____

_____

STEP 2 Questions

Is that fear preventing you from choosing a period of abstinence? Or is there something else?

The 4 STEPS

What other fears or losses do you associate with abstinence?

THE CHALLENGE

If someone challenged you to a period of abstinence, how long do you think you could abstain from the substance(s) or behavior(s)? Do you think you could last longer once you got started?

_____

_____

_____

_____

_____

_____

_____

_____

_____

_____

_____

_____

_____

_____

_____

The 4 STEPS

Do you believe you can do it? What would be your biggest motivator for accepting the challenge?

_____

_____

_____

_____

_____

_____

_____

_____

_____

_____

_____

_____

_____

_____

_____

_____

STEP 2 Questions

What benefits would you gain by accepting the challenge of your own free will instead of being shamed or pressured into it by others?

The 4 STEPS

Do you have resources to help you during the period of abstinence? If not, do you know someone or a group that could help support you? (A friend, mentor, organization, church or spiritual group.)

_____

_____

_____

_____

_____

_____

_____

_____

_____

_____

_____

_____

_____

_____

_____

STEP 2 Questions

MAKING A DECISION

Has STEP 1 prepared you to make a personal decision about abstinence? If so, how? If not, why not? (Be specific.)

The 4 STEPS

How do you see your relationship with God/Love/The Universe being strengthened through a period of abstinence?

STEP 2 Questions

What do you personally want to gain by making the choice to abstain from your addiction(s)?

_____

_____

_____

_____

_____

_____

_____

_____

_____

_____

_____

_____

_____

_____

_____

_____

The 4 STEPS

During this period of abstinence, what would you like to eliminate from your life? Can you imagine eliminating it forever?

___
___
___
___
___
___
___
___
___
___
___
___
___
___
___
___

STEP 2 Questions

How will making the decision to abstain from your addiction(s) empower you?

_____
_____
_____
_____
_____
_____
_____
_____
_____
_____
_____
_____
_____
_____
_____
_____
_____

STEP 3

**Change Your Environment:
Walk Away from Your Triggers**

> It's the past.
> Leave it there,
> Or it will never leave you.
> —*Moving Past the Past*, A.D. Burks
> From *Sex and Surrender: An Addict's Journey*

Change Your Environment: Walk Away from Your Triggers

We have come to STEP 3, the halfway point. I say "we" because you are not alone in this journey and it's so important you know that. You are one STEP closer to breaking the addictive cycle that has created so much chaos in your life, the lives of the people you love and who love you, and even the lives of innocent bystanders. Making the decision of abstinence in STEP 2 provides a great segue to the work necessary for STEP 3, which is to better understand yourself and your triggers.

To change your environment, you first have to become conscious of what is surrounding you. Because we are creatures of habit, it's easy to become numb to things around us, whether they are detrimental or beneficial. In STEP 3 we will focus on the ways in which we become accustomed to destructive patterns and come to see them as normal. The only way to really assess what it will take to change the negative influences in your environment is to first determine what those influences are. Only then can you to figure out what is triggering your addictive cycle.

Who

It is hard to overestimate the importance of the company we keep. When I was deep in the addictive cycle I kept other addicts around me, and they helped bring out the worst in me. It makes me sad to admit this, but we would compete to see who could have sex with the most people in a given night. But it helps me to acknowledge the people who were influencing me then, and to see their contribution to my addictive cycle.

Addicts of a Feather Flock Together

Ultimately, I had to take responsibility and accountability for my actions. No one forced me to engage in that behavior; I chose it of my own free will. Just as I chose to associate with those people to get my addictive fix, I had to intentionally separate from them to break my addictive cycle.

Logically, in order to get to a healthier place, it might seem to make sense to disassociate from people who encourage destructive behavior, but emotionally and psychologically, it is counterintuitive. The neurological pathways in my brain had associated pleasure with these individuals. And now I had to make a conscious decision to distance myself. At first, it was

STEP 3

extremely difficult: these people were interwoven into the fabric of my life. I had laughed and even cried with some of them, but with most of them I had acted out, and that is what I had to keep in the forefront of my mind.

When I informed a few of my addict friends that I would have to stop hanging out at bars and clubs (because those were typically the places where we acted out), they thought something was wrong with me. "Does he think he's better than us?" one so-called friend asked. It's quite telling to realize who my real friends were: those who encouraged me to improve myself even when they chose to continue their addictive behavior. And those who talked behind my back and spread vicious and untrue rumors—they were not my friends.

Taking inventory of the people I chose to keep in my life was crucial to starting the process of changing my environment.

Why, What and When

Pain

After I assessed who helped trigger my addictive cycle, I needed to figure out why I was being triggered. One of the main themes in my memoir *Sex and Surrender: An Addict's Journey* is that *Addiction = Pain.*

Pain comes in various forms: physical, mental, emotional and

117

spiritual. As a society, we generally give credence to physical pain, but the other types of pain can be just as debilitating, maybe even more so, because the mind controls the body.

When I felt pain—primarily, intense emotional pain—I found myself seeking ways to act out sexually. Sex served as an escape from the pain. So I had to ask myself the following questions: What was causing the pain and when was this intense emotional pain most acute?

Shame

In *Daring Greatly,* Brene Brown provides great insight on shame and the way being shamed affects us. By being in therapy, I discovered that one of the root causes of my addiction was my inability to accept my sexuality. My religious upbringing and society in general taught me that homosexuality was wrong, and that meant that *I* was wrong, a reality that caused me great shame. To deal with the intense shame, I acted out sexually.

People Pleasing and Rejection

I'm the last person most people would consider to be a people pleaser. When I was a kid, my mom always used to say, "If they aren't paying your bills, don't worry about what they say!" It was a saying I took to heart, and that allowed me to accomplish things others couldn't because they were so worried about what people might think of them. It has been especially beneficial to me in the business world. I can easily discern the difference between taking things personally and simply letting other matters be business matters.

But when I was dealing with the person who was paying my bills, my mom, and the people I love, it was a totally different story. God's favor on my life and my mother's sacrifice are the primary reasons why I have achieved what I have. I will never forget the endless hours my mom invested in my education, the way she exposed me to different cultures and experiences, and the fact that she made sure I had the best possible life that she could afford to give me.

And yet there was a key problem: my mom and others whom I love believed (and some still believe) that I should be married to a woman. Given their religious beliefs and other cultural norms, they believed that if I were married to a woman I would have the best chance at having the family they envisioned for me. I know that deep down they had my best interests at heart, but that doesn't mean their vision for my life is what is best for me. So I waged an internal battle: I didn't believe I could have a family with a man, and yet I was attracted to men; I listened to the people who loved me, and they believed I needed to be with a woman.

I worked so hard at trying to please the people I love;

eventually, I would become so frustrated that I needed to find a way to deal with the pain. What I was experiencing was both actual and perceived rejection. Some of the people I loved most held strong beliefs, and I felt that if they knew the truth about my sexuality, they wouldn't love me anymore. I would be rejected and I didn't stand a chance of being loved for who I truly was. And that's when I would act out sexually. It seemed like everybody was getting their needs met but me.

Hopelessness

I didn't believe there was a way out, and that meant I would have to live the rest of my life as a lie. These beliefs intensified the addiction. Because I could see no way out, I sought relief from that pain by acting out. Essentially, my primary need was to be loved unconditionally by someone I desired and loved, and in an attempt to meet that need I used sex. I'd find someone who wanted me sexually and I'd engage in sex, hoping to satisfy my need to be loved. But here is the reality: SEX ≠ LOVE

An Impossible Dream

When my parents got divorced, I felt abandoned by my father. As a child, I always dreamed of having a "normal" family—i.e., someone I loved who loved me, plus a couple of kids. When I saw other men my age who had families of their own, I felt as if I would never realize my dream of having a family of my own. To be honest, I was genuinely happy for those men and I wasn't jealous, but I was unhappy. The emotional pain would kick in and I'd use sex to relieve it. If I couldn't have the family I wanted, at least I'd have great sex with someone I wanted.

Not Getting My Way

I was an only child, one who was extremely blessed to have two parents who truly loved me. I also had non-biological grandparents who would spoil me when they came to Texas or when I visited them in Tennessee. In short, I was used to getting what I wanted, when I wanted it.

Academically, I was pretty astute. Advanced classes and a heavy academic workload were the norm for me during middle and high school. My hard work paid off and I graduated at the top of my class and received numerous academic scholarships, earning my undergraduate degree in less than four years.

I don't bring up these things to boast or tell you how great I am; I know my gifts and talents come from God and are also a result of my mom's sacrifices. Instead, I'm building a case for what turned out to be a vulnerable point for me: when I didn't get my way, I didn't know how to handle it. I believed that when you worked hard, you reaped the reward, but when that didn't happen, I was devastated.

After I graduated from Grinnell College with a degree in

Chemistry, I embarked on a professional singing career. I wanted to be an international superstar. My journey in search of stardom took me to Nashville, then to Atlanta, and finally backed to Houston. I learned some key life lessons along the way (I relate these in detail in my memoir *Sex and Surrender: An Addict's Journey*).

My breaking point came after I assembled a band with my manager and spent countless hours in rehearsal as I prepared to sing at a showcase for Warner Brothers Records in New York. I had written great lyrics; I and the producers had worked very hard; we had assembled amazing musicians and backup singers. And yet the rehearsals were not going well. From the time I was four years old, I had performed countless live concerts with different choirs, but I didn't have experience singing solo with a live band.

When the time came for me to perform the live showcase, my manager knew I wasn't ready. She told me, "the crowd will eat you alive." I can barely express how devastated and defeated I was to hear those words. I couldn't dismiss what she said—she believed in me and supported me, but what she said was true. When it came to performing, I was used to being instructed, but with a live band I had to do the instructing. At that moment, I had to face reality and I knew my hopes and dreams of being an international singing star were over.

So what was I supposed to do? I had put my heart and soul, time, talent and money into making my dream come true. From childhood I had been taught that if I did the work I would get the reward. And I had seen that play out in my life. But what I wanted most wasn't happening. I experienced every negative emotional state one could have—disappointment, grief, and rage were waiting for me on the other side of my unrealized dream. I was learning one of the most difficult and painful lessons of my life: I wasn't in total control of my world.

To regain a sense of control I turned to sex. Since I wasn't getting my way, sex was one thing I believed I could control and that would allow me to feel empowered. Any time I used sex to escape the pain of not getting my way, I was feeding the addict. I wasn't yet ready for STEP 1—accepting that God had a better plan for my life and that I needed to be patient.

I know now that if I had realized my dream of becoming an international singing superstar, I may well have self-destructed, because I still hadn't accepted my sexuality, or dealt with my abandonment issues or my need to please the people I love. Now I'm grateful that my dream didn't come true because I wouldn't have had the chance to share the lessons I've learned with others. I have to keep reminding myself: **God knows best.** Just because I'm not getting exactly what I want right now doesn't mean it's not going to happen.

The 4 STEPS

How

Once I was able to see the emotional and psychological patterns that were causing me to act out, I needed to focus on *how* I acted out. It became critical for me to see that an initial instance of acting out could lead to other ways of acting out. If I could catch myself at the outset, it was more likely that I could prevent a total addictive binge.

My typical addictive pattern started with watching porn. The internet has transformed the pornography industry and allowed immediate access, which has increased the susceptibility to porn addiction/sex addiction. Porn is such a pervasive trigger and it is easily accessible and free.

When I felt overwhelmed, I'd seek out various forms of porn to masturbate to. But with my Type A personality, it wasn't enough for me to simply watch others having sex. After viewing porn, typically my next stop would be a bar or club because I needed to find someone with whom I could act out sexually. The initial trigger of watching porn escalated to another trigger. And that's how the downward spiral begins.

If I couldn't find someone I wanted to have sex with at the bars and clubs, my last resort would be a bathhouse. Each trigger would lead me deeper into my addiction, putting my mental, physical and emotional health at risk. Thankfully, God kept me safe in those potentially disastrous situations. So now

STEP 3

I see it as my responsibility to make sure I understand what my triggers are and to help others determine theirs, so the addictive cycle can be broken.

STEP 3 QUESTIONS

I was intentionally candid about my addiction here, providing some detail about whom, why, what, when and how I was triggered, and I hope that my disclosure might encourage you to look at what your own triggers are. Really examine your unique situation: What triggers someone else may have no effect on you, or vice versa. The key is doing an honest self-inventory.

A number of factors from your childhood and past may contribute to why certain people, places, things and emotions trigger your urge to act out. Those factors can't be changed, but what *can* be changed is your awareness of what triggers you and your ability to create a plan to avoid or handle those triggers when they can't be avoided.

The following questions are intended to help you determine what your triggers are and what patterns you tend to follow that may lead you to act out.

The 4 STEPS

WHO

Who is around you when you want to act out?

___

STEP 3 Questions

Is there something that this person(s) says or does that makes you want to act out? If so, what is it?

The 4 STEPS

Who is around you when you engage in your addiction? (List potential enablers)

STEP 3 Questions

Do they struggle with the same addiction? (Addicts of a feather flock together)

The 4 STEPS

If so, when do you typically get together? Where do you meet or hang out?

STEP 3 Questions

WHY, WHAT AND WHEN

Pain
What source(s) of pain are you dealing with? (Physical, mental, or spiritual)

_____

_____

_____

_____

_____

_____

_____

_____

_____

_____

_____

_____

_____

_____

_____

The 4 STEPS

What levels of severity (low, moderate or extreme) do you experience on a given day, week or month?

STEP 3 Questions

As best you can, describe in detail the pain for each level and/or time period.

The 4 STEPS

What do you do and/or use to escape the pain?

_____

_____

_____

_____

_____

_____

_____

_____

_____

_____

_____

_____

_____

_____

STEP 3 Questions

Is there someone who engaged in this same behavior to escape pain? Was it a parent, family member, friend, or someone you admired? (This question is meant to help you identify a connection or pattern, and is not intended to blame another person or eliminate your personal responsibility.)

_____
_____
_____
_____
_____
_____
_____
_____
_____
_____
_____
_____
_____
_____
_____

The 4 STEPS

SHAME

List attributes, behavior or actions of which you are ashamed.

_____

_____

_____

_____

_____

_____

_____

_____

_____

_____

_____

_____

_____

_____

_____

_____

_____

STEP 3 Questions

What are you most ashamed of?

The 4 STEPS

Do family members, friends, co-workers, and/or enemies know these aspects of who you are?

STEP 3 Questions

If they know, what comments have they made, and how did those comments make you feel? If they don't know, what is your biggest fear about them finding out?

_____

_____

_____

_____

_____

_____

_____

_____

_____

_____

_____

_____

_____

_____

_____

_____

_____

The 4 STEPS

PEOPLE PLEASING AND REJECTION

List the individuals or groups/organizations you want to please.

_____

_____

_____

_____

_____

_____

_____

_____

_____

_____

_____

_____

_____

_____

_____

_____

STEP 3 Questions

Why do you want to please them?

_____
_____
_____
_____
_____
_____
_____
_____
_____
_____
_____
_____
_____
_____
_____
_____
_____
_____
_____

The 4 STEPS

If you were to please them, could you still be yourself? Explain.

_____
_____
_____
_____
_____
_____
_____
_____
_____
_____
_____
_____
_____
_____
_____
_____
_____

STEP 3 Questions

What would happen if you stopped trying to please them?

___

The 4 STEPS

If you stopped trying to please them, would you still feel loved? If not, why not? Is it because of what you believe or because of something they've said or done in the past? Explain in detail.

_____

_____

_____

_____

_____

_____

_____

_____

_____

_____

_____

_____

_____

_____

_____

STEP 3 Questions

Describe a past situation in which you were rejected by someone you love or loved, focusing on the pain it caused.

The 4 STEPS

Think about a person who rejected you. Is it possible for you to get that person's approval? If it is not possible, do you believe that you can still pursue the life you want? If not, why not?

_____

_____

_____

_____

_____

_____

_____

_____

_____

_____

_____

_____

_____

_____

_____

HOPELESSNESS

What do you believe you cannot change about yourself and/or about your life?

_____
_____
_____
_____
_____
_____
_____
_____
_____
_____
_____
_____
_____
_____
_____
_____

The 4 STEPS

How do you cope with what you cannot change?

STEP 3 Questions

Have you spoken with a professional (therapist, counselor, minister, psychologist, or psychiatrist) about this? If so, how did the person respond? If you have not spoken with a professional, why not?

_____

_____

_____

_____

_____

_____

_____

_____

_____

_____

_____

_____

_____

_____

The 4 STEPS

AN IMPOSSIBLE DREAM

What dream(s) have you not yet achieved?

_____

_____

_____

_____

_____

_____

_____

_____

_____

_____

_____

_____

_____

_____

_____

_____

STEP 3 Questions

Describe in detail the plan you have developed to make your dream(s) a reality. If you haven't created a plan, what resources do you need to establish one?

_____

_____

_____

_____

_____

_____

_____

_____

_____

_____

_____

_____

_____

_____

_____

The 4 STEPS

What are you doing daily, weekly or monthly towards that plan?

_____

_____

_____

_____

_____

_____

_____

_____

_____

_____

_____

_____

_____

_____

_____

_____

STEP 3 Questions

If your established plan has not worked, what adjustments can you make? Have you spoken with someone who has achieved that particular dream or a similar dream?

_____
_____
_____
_____
_____
_____
_____
_____
_____
_____
_____
_____
_____
_____
_____
_____

The 4 STEPS

If your dream hasn't come to fruition after you've done all you can, have you tuned in to what God or divine wisdom has to say to you about that particular dream? (If you haven't asked the divine, consider doing that right now and write down what you hear in your spirit.)

_____

_____

_____

_____

_____

_____

_____

_____

_____

_____

_____

_____

_____

_____

_____

STEP 3 Questions

In your spirit, do you believe you deserve to be happy? If not, why not?

_____
_____
_____
_____
_____
_____
_____
_____
_____
_____
_____
_____
_____
_____
_____
_____
_____
_____
_____

The 4 STEPS

What does happiness look like for you?

___

STEP 3 Questions

NOT GETTING YOUR WAY

What do you do when you don't get your way?

The 4 STEPS

Do you believe your way is always or is generally the best way? If your answer is "yes," can you think of a time when it has not been? Was there someone who suggested or provided a better way?

_____

_____

_____

_____

_____

_____

_____

_____

_____

_____

_____

_____

_____

_____

STEP 3 Questions

What have you done in the past when you felt your way was better than God's way?

The 4 STEPS

When you cannot be patient, what do you do?

STEP 3 Questions

Is there something you could do instead that would help you grow in the area of patience and spiritually?

The 4 STEPS

HOW

Once your pain reaches the initial threshold of discomfort, what is the first way you try to escape? (Be very specific.)

_____

_____

_____

_____

_____

_____

_____

_____

_____

_____

_____

_____

_____

STEP 3 Questions

When that initial escape doesn't suffice, what do you do next and after that?

The 4 STEPS

If that second, third or fourth escape method doesn't ultimately relieve the pain, what do you do?

_____
_____
_____
_____
_____
_____
_____
_____
_____
_____
_____
_____
_____
_____
_____
_____

STEP 3 Questions

List in sequential order how you act out your addictive cycle.

Now that you know the sequence of your addictive cycle, what can you do at each point along the cycle to make an intervention in an addictive binge? (Maybe call someone, pray, or remove yourself from a particular person or environment.)

_____

_____

_____

_____

_____

_____

_____

_____

_____

_____

_____

_____

_____

_____

_____

STEP 4

Establish a Support Network

In solitude, I was forced to confront who I had become.
Yearning to become the man I was called,
I look to You for guidance.
—*Rock Bottom, A.D. Burks*
From *Sex and Surrender: An Addict's Journey*

Establish a Support Network

No doubt you've heard the saying that no man is an island. I'd like to add that no one can break an addiction by himself or herself. Life and humanity is about social interaction. The sole reason I've spent countless hours writing about how I was able to break my addictive cycle is because I know that God wanted me to help other people. Help from others is exactly what STEP 4 is about. If it hadn't been for my support network, there is no doubt in my mind that I would still be struggling with my addiction. It's the secretive nature of addiction that keeps the addict isolated and feeling that there is no way out.

The last step, which is just as important as the previous three steps, is establishing the right support network. Unfortunately, not everyone has your best interests at heart. Many people are struggling with their own addictions, past hurts and childhood wounds. So you must be prudent when selecting who will be a part of your support network. The spiritual work you completed in STEP 1 will help you listen to what God is saying about who really belongs in your support network. God will place those people in your life if they aren't already there. At this point, if you have completed STEP 3 you have removed the people you identified as helping to enable your addictive cycle. If you haven't yet broken away from those individuals, please go back to STEP 3 and complete that process. One way to identify those enablers: they are likely the people who will discount and discredit what a true support network will say to help you along the process of breaking your addiction. Ultimately, the choice is yours.

Once I realized that I needed a support network of people I could go to when I needed a word of encouragement, a shoulder to cry on or someone to tell me when I was wrong, I thought about the qualities and character traits these people might have. Obviously, I had to be able to trust them. When I looked deeper, there were many qualities that contributed to me being able to trust a person with something that was so personal and life-changing.

Spirituality

It all goes back to STEP 1. If a person doesn't have a personal relationship with God, how can I know what they are telling me is spiritually influenced and right for me? When I look at

STEP 4

the people in my support network, every single one is spiritual. When I say "spiritual," I don't mean religious. They don't all go to church, but they do have a personal relationship with God.

How do I know? When a person is spiritual, she is able to convey what God has done for her that she couldn't have done by herself and to describe the effect it had on her life. She will say or do something for you that you know only God could have ordained at a specific moment in time. In short, you'll connect with that person on a spiritual plane/realm. The work you did in STEP 1 should have opened your spirit up to that place.

Two members in my support network are ordained and theologically trained ministers who have been instrumental in supporting me during the most pivotal moments in my journey of accepting my sexuality, which was vital in getting to the root of my addiction. The first is my best friend; we attended high school and college together. He explained the controversial passage in Leviticus regarding homosexuality being an abomination. He said that the text was taken from a period when God was trying to grow a nation, and so any sex that did not lead to reproduction was considered to be an abomination.

This insight led me to look deeper into what I had been taught and had blindly believed about the passage.

That addressed the Old Testament's teaching on sexuality, but the New Testament addressed it as well, or at least I believed it had, but that was because I didn't really understand the terminology. Another close confidante and spiritual leader educated me to the fact that the word "homosexual" wasn't originally used in the New Testament. The word was "catamite." After I looked up the definition and determined that there was a clear difference between a boy who has a sexual relationship with a man and a man who expresses his love sexually with another man, I no longer believed that homosexuality was a sin.

These two crucial insights changed my perception of myself and my perception of others. If it hadn't been for these two people in my support network, I might still be struggling with my sexuality. My religion proclaimed that my sexuality was an abomination and that I was going to hell, and my acceptance of that view was one of the main contributors to my addiction. Given my religious upbringing, I have no question that God knew I would need someone trained in theology to help me navigate the misguided beliefs I held about myself in order to break my addictive cycle.

STEP 4

Addiction-Free

Just because a person is spiritual doesn't mean they're above being an addict. And just because someone is spiritual doesn't mean they should be in your support network while you're battling your addictive cycle. During the height of my addiction, I still went to church, a practice that was more religious than spiritual. From a spiritual standpoint, I was wrestling with being obedient to what God was telling me and trying to find a way to escape the pain I was experiencing.

If a person is currently struggling with addiction, how can he or she advise you on breaking your own addiction? It's like the addict leading the addict. Even if the person is giving you good advice, it's easy to dismiss it because you know he or she is struggling with an addiction.

I know that many support networks and organizations pair mentors or sponsors with those who have previously battled with the same addiction, but I found it more beneficial to have people in my support network who hadn't been sex addicts. When I attended certain sex addiction recovery meetings, I found that listening to other addicts recount their stories exposed me to new ways of acting out. Instead of providing a place for support and healing, the meeting inadvertently became a place to be triggered.

It has been proven that what you focus on is what you move toward. When I had weak moments in which I fell back into the addictive cycle or wanted to act out, I'd call members of my support network who weren't addicts and they refocused me on my future, my goals and my purpose. Instead of reliving a negative and destructive past, I was focused on a healthy and more productive future.

Being Unselfish

Today we give so much attention to the "me, me, me" personality and mentality. It's no wonder the family and friendships are in disarray and addictions are on the rise. But to break the addictive cycle I needed people who were concerned about things other than themselves. I needed unselfish friends, mentors and family members.

Selfish people don't have time to help you in your time of need. They're too busy trying to purchase the next house, or the newest car, or get a reservation at the trendiest restaurant or club. Do any of these scenarios sound familiar? They should because it's what television is constantly telling us is valuable by idolizing celebrities.

What really matters, though, are people who know that they're not on this earth just to see what they can get but also what they can give. These are the ones who know that the only way things will get better is if we work together for the greater good no matter what a person's race, ethnicity, religion, sexual orientation, financial status, or addiction.

There are so many ways that selfishness is evident and it is also something we go to great lengths to hide. So I had to be vigilant about detecting even the slightest hint of selfishness in people I initially decided to discuss my addiction with. Being an addict makes you selfish, so I really had to make sure to eliminate selfish people from my support network.

Honesty

Another prevalent trend is telling "little lies." It might be a businesswoman who isn't completely forthright about the terms of a deal, and so lying by omission, in order to land a new account; or it might be something as simple as a man taking office supplies home to help his children with their schoolwork. We can all justify why we chose to do what we did, but ultimately, we are not being honest.

When capital gain is considered nobler than telling the truth, dishonesty permeates our culture at an endemic level. Yet politicians, special interest groups and everyday hypocrites preach family values when what they're doing runs counter to their message. It's no wonder why hate holds a permanent place in our schools, religious institutions and work environments.

Of course, everyone isn't like that and there is hope. Some people believe that being anything other than completely honest is being dishonest. Some view compassion as more important than temporary financial gain. And they are the people I needed to support me in breaking my addictive cycle.

These people couldn't be swayed by appearances because they knew that I was hurting myself and others. I knew that when I spoke to them I would get unadulterated truth, which is what I needed to hear. The only way to be free from the addictive cycle is by being honest with yourself. When you're surrounded with dishonest people who are running from their own truth, it isn't likely that you'll be able to recognize the truth.

Trustworthiness

While a person may be honest, that doesn't necessarily mean he or she is trustworthy. There are "blatantly honest" people who cannot be trusted. Any information they receive goes out for general consumption within minutes. When I was building my support network, I made sure I found people who were trustworthy.

A trustworthy person is one whom I can tell my most intimate fears to without a second thought about anyone else getting that information. A trustworthy person is one whom I can give a blank check and know he or she will never write it for a single penny over what we agreed on. That's the level of trust I needed from people in my support network.

Now there are levels of trustworthiness. Some people extend trust to anyone until someone proves they can't be trusted. Other people don't trust anyone until they pass a series of tests. Personally, I take the former approach. Some friends I trust with a majority of information, but I know the extent to which I can truly trust them. I genuinely appreciate the level of trust we have established. But there are only two friends who I trust blindly, and they both have known me for years and have proven to be trustworthy beyond belief.

Being Protective

When I was struggling with my addiction, having members of my support network who were protective of me was invaluable. These friends knew my weaknesses and were protective of me even when I wasn't protective of myself.

In my memoir I wrote about a friend who, when I revealed to him that I was at a bar where most people hooked up, told me to go home three different times. He knew that if I stayed there

I would have acted out and gone back into an addictive cycle. I listened to him, and I was so grateful he called me that night. Given the state I was in at that moment, I might have engaged in some activities that could have endangered me.

Now there is a difference between protective and being controlling. The former entails advice and suggestion while the latter entails force. It can be a fine line, but when it is crossed it can be detrimental. If you allow someone to control you, you ultimately become dependent on them, and that can lead to codependency, another form of addiction. We all need to be careful and to realize that we are ultimately responsible for ourselves. Your support network is there to support you, not to parent you.

Empathy

In today's world of Selfies, self-promotion, self-centeredness and lack of self-awareness, empathy can be hard to find. We're so self-absorbed that we don't even take into account the ways that someone else might be affected: to really think about another person's struggle takes considerable effort. When I was struggling with my addiction, there were times I was incapable of looking outside myself. I like to say that I have OCS—Only Child Syndrome—and that can make it more difficult for me to be empathetic as well. While I genuinely cared about people who were unable to help themselves, I was less tolerant of those who constantly made excuses. Since I didn't really have anyone besides my mother I could totally depend on, I became very self-reliant. If I encountered someone who had two parents and siblings as well, I just assumed that they didn't need any support. It took me a while to learn that just because someone had biological relatives didn't mean they automatically had support.

Thankfully, I had a support network that gave me what I wasn't able to give during my addiction: empathy. They were able to look past their own personal challenges and see a friend who was in pain and give of their time. Whether it was just listening or giving constructive feedback in a loving manner, their ability to empathize with what I was going through was critical to my recovery.

Integrity

The best definition I heard for integrity came from a relationship therapist. He said that integrity was doing what you say you're going to do, except and unless it has become totally impossible, in which case you make a satisfactory amends. WOW! That definition blew me away. From childhood, my mother had instilled that concept in me, yet I had never heard it defined as integrity. For me, if someone didn't follow through on what they said they were going to do, I just considered them a liar. At the very least, I just assumed that they didn't have as much integrity as I did.

Part of the addictive cycle is feeling isolated and alone, so creating a support network of people who have great integrity is paramount. These are the people who say, "You can call me anytime of the night," and actually mean it. I found this out the hard way: there were plenty of people who said that I could call them if I needed anything, but when I called they didn't answer and never returned my call.

Integrity also extends to being able to articulate your limits and to being able to say no. Instead of claiming that they could do something or be somewhere at a certain time, I had close friends with praiseworthy levels of integrity who would say, "I can't be there tomorrow, but I can be there the next day." That was exactly the level of integrity I needed when I was feeling alone. I might not be able to get my need met immediately, but I knew it would be met by someone with integrity.

Accountability

The word most addicts don't want to hear but need to hear the most is *accountability.* One of the key components of breaking my sex addiction was a support network of people who held me accountable. When I wanted to watch porn, one of my main triggers, they would be the people reminding me of what that activity could lead to. While it might not have been what I wanted to hear in the moment, it was exactly what I needed to hear.

People who were accountable themselves had an easier time holding me accountable. All I had to do was look at their life and see how they were flourishing by being addiction-free. And when people didn't hold themselves accountable for their actions, it was a bit tougher to listen to them reminding me of the ways I needed to be accountable. Even if they didn't do as they said, it was at least good to know that they wanted me to do as I said. Having people in my support network who made accountability a priority was mandatory.

Resourcefulness

For me personally, being resourceful and being creative go hand-in-hand. We have a litany of excuses for not taking action and not accomplishing our goals. We all have limitations, and it is tempting to make excuses. But those were not the kind of people I needed in my support network. Successful people know how to take what God has given them and make something out of it.

Here is one of the things I appreciate most about myself: I know that I don't know all the answers, but I'm willing to find someone who does. That particular trait has allowed me to learn so much and seek out opportunities that have made me a better person. That resourcefulness is what I looked for in people in my support network.

You often hear people say that they don't have money for therapy, but there are organizations that offer free counseling, as well as associations whose mission it is to help the less fortunate. The key is to leave the excuses/rationale behind and start searching. *Seek and ye shall find.* Find resourceful people who want to see you become the best person you can be—that's living addiction-free!

STEP 4 QUESTIONS

I hope the framework I provided to show how I determined who I wanted in my support network helps you to better evaluate who should be in yours. These parameters were helpful to me, so feel free to take what you want and add to it. The most important thing is to remember to listen to for God's guidance when making your decisions.

A key aspect of a support network is giving. Even at times when I was deep in an addictive cycle, I was able to help support people in my network. The level of support definitely wasn't the same, and probably didn't look the same, as the kind of support I have been able to provide once I was living addiction-free, but the support was there. The key to a network is to be able to both give support and to accept it from others. No network will work if its members are only taking.

Here are some questions that might help you assess the characteristics and traits of the people you choose for your support network.

The 4 STEPS

SPIRITUALITY

If we define "spiritual" as having an intimate and personal relationship with God, then is this person spiritual? How do you know?

_____

_____

_____

_____

_____

_____

_____

_____

_____

_____

_____

_____

_____

_____

_____

STEP 4 Questions

Was there a time when you felt that God might be using this person as a way to speak to you? If so, what happened?

The 4 STEPS

Do you connect with this person on a spiritual plane? If so, how?

_____

_____

_____

_____

_____

_____

_____

_____

_____

_____

_____

_____

_____

_____

_____

_____

_____

_____

STEP 4 Questions

Given the work you did in STEP 1, do you see any parallels between this person's spirituality and that work? What are they? (I encourage you to go back and review your answers from STEP 1.)

ADDICTION-FREE

Is the person(s) you choose for your support network currently struggling with the same addiction you are? If not, are they struggling with another addiction? Which one?

_____
_____
_____
_____
_____
_____
_____
_____
_____
_____
_____
_____
_____
_____
_____

STEP 4 Questions

Whether or not the person is struggling with an addiction, do you trust him or her to point out when you are in your addictive cycle or about to head into it? If so, why or why not?

___

The 4 STEPS

Have you attended support meetings for your particular addiction (food, drugs, alcohol, sex, etc.) and found yourself being triggered by some of the discussions? If so, what was said? Who said it?

_____

_____

_____

_____

_____

_____

_____

_____

_____

_____

_____

_____

_____

_____

_____

STEP 4 Questions

In the meetings are there any recurring themes that inadvertently trigger you? What are they?

_____
_____
_____
_____
_____
_____
_____
_____
_____
_____
_____
_____
_____
_____
_____

The 4 STEPS

BEING UNSELFISH

When this person is presented with a choice between helping someone and doing something unproductive, which do they choose?

_____

_____

_____

_____

_____

_____

_____

_____

_____

_____

_____

_____

_____

_____

STEP 4 Questions

Is the only time you hear from this person when he or she needs something or when it's convenient for him or her? (List examples.)

_____
_____
_____
_____
_____
_____
_____
_____
_____
_____
_____
_____
_____
_____
_____
_____

The 4 STEPS

When you have a conversation, is it a monologue or a dialogue? Who does the conversation usually center around—you, her/him or both of you?

_____

_____

_____

_____

_____

_____

_____

_____

_____

_____

_____

_____

_____

_____

_____

_____

_____

STEP 4 Questions

What are this person's highest goals and dreams? (List them.)
Does he or she know your main goals and dreams?

The 4 STEPS

Has this person taken the time to know what your triggers are and suggested or helped devise a plan to keep you away from those triggers? If so, what is the plan?

_____

_____

_____

_____

_____

_____

_____

_____

_____

_____

_____

_____

_____

_____

STEP 4 Questions

HONESTY

Have you knowingly caught this person in a lie? What was the lie?

The 4 STEPS

Did you confront him or her? Why or why not?

STEP 4 Questions

What was the person's rationale? How did the explanation make you feel?

_____

_____

_____

_____

_____

_____

_____

_____

_____

_____

_____

_____

_____

_____

_____

_____

_____

_____

The 4 STEPS

Have honest people you know suggested that this person is dishonest? If so, why?

___

STEP 4 Questions

Has there been a time where he or she didn't have to be honest but choose to be anyway? Explain. (For example: received too much change from a cashier and chose to return it.)

_____

_____

_____

_____

_____

_____

_____

_____

_____

_____

_____

_____

_____

_____

_____

_____

_____

The 4 STEPS

TRUSTWORTHINESS

Is this person(s) able to keep confidential information confidential? (Give a personal example.)

STEP 4 Questions

Have you ever told this person one of your most intimate secrets? Which one(s)? If you haven't, why not?

The 4 STEPS

How do you approach trust? Do you trust a person until they prove they can't be trusted, or do you trust a person only once they prove they can be trusted? What advantages and disadvantages have you seen by using that approach?

_____

_____

_____

_____

_____

_____

_____

_____

_____

_____

_____

_____

_____

_____

STEP 4 Questions

What aspects of the opposite approach might be beneficial for you to incorporate?

The 4 STEPS

BEING PROTECTIVE

Has this person(s) let you know when it was time for you to get out of an environment that could lead you back to your addictive cycle? If so, when?

_____

_____

_____

_____

_____

_____

_____

_____

_____

_____

_____

_____

_____

_____

_____

_____

STEP 4 Questions

When someone has said something untrue about you, would this person speak up and come to your defense? Has he or she done so in the past? When? If the person didn't speak up, why didn't he or she do so?

_____

_____

_____

_____

_____

_____

_____

_____

_____

_____

_____

_____

_____

_____

_____

The 4 STEPS

In the past, has this person(s) tried to coerce you into a decision or plan? Or has she or he suggested options or choices instead? (Give examples.)

___

STEP 4 Questions

EMPATHY

How do you define empathy and what does it look like to you?

_____

_____

_____

_____

_____

_____

_____

_____

_____

_____

_____

_____

_____

_____

_____

The 4 STEPS

Give an example of how this person(s) has demonstrated empathy with you and others?

_____

_____

_____

_____

_____

_____

_____

_____

_____

_____

_____

_____

_____

_____

_____

STEP 4 Questions

What type of stance does this person take regarding issues that don't directly relate to him or her? (For example: hate crimes, gay marriage, equal pay, immigration, animal rights, etc.)

_____

_____

_____

_____

_____

_____

_____

_____

_____

_____

_____

_____

_____

_____

_____

_____

_____

The 4 STEPS

INTEGRITY

Think of the last time this person did not follow through on his or her word. What happened?

STEP 4 Questions

Did he or she do anything to make amends? If so what? If not, what could he or she do now to make amends or for you to feel validated?

The 4 STEPS

Give an example of a circumstance in which you displayed praiseworthy integrity. Would the people in your support network do something similar? If not, explain why they are in your support network.

_____

_____

_____

_____

_____

_____

_____

_____

_____

_____

_____

_____

_____

_____

_____

_____

ACCOUNTABILITY

Give an example(s) of how the people in your support network have proven to be accountable.

_____

_____

_____

_____

_____

_____

_____

_____

_____

_____

_____

_____

_____

_____

_____

The 4 STEPS

How have these people held you accountable in the past? (Be specific.)

_____

_____

_____

_____

_____

_____

_____

_____

_____

_____

_____

_____

_____

_____

_____

_____

STEP 4 Questions

What do you need to do now for them to hold you accountable so that you can take the necessary steps to break your addiction?

_____

_____

_____

_____

_____

_____

_____

_____

_____

_____

_____

_____

_____

_____

The 4 STEPS

RESOURCEFULNESS

How often does this person(s) make excuses for why something didn't happen or go the way he or she said it would? (Always, Rarely, Never.)

STEP 4 Questions

Does he or she typically have a reason/excuse for why things do not go as planned? (For example: it's someone else's fault, he or she doesn't have enough resources or enough time, etc.) Give specific examples.

_____
_____
_____
_____
_____
_____
_____
_____
_____
_____
_____
_____
_____
_____
_____
_____
_____

The 4 STEPS

When this person is challenged to do something he or she has never done before, how does he or she respond? Be specific.

STEP 4 Questions

Explain a circumstance in which this person(s) was required to complete a task that required him or her to organize resources not at his or her immediate disposal. What happened? Would you hire this person? Why or why not?

_____

_____

_____

_____

_____

_____

_____

_____

_____

_____

_____

_____

_____

_____

_____

_____

CONCLUSION

I hope I'm not the only one to convey this, but I want you to know how incredibly proud you should be for taking the time to do the necessary work to break your addictive cycle. I pray that by engaging with The 4 STEPS workbook you've opened your mind to the endless possibilities life has to offer and are better able to experience those possibilities addiction-free. Many addicts want to end their addiction, and some even embark on that path, but you've done the necessary work to break the cycle.

I know it wasn't easy. There were probably times you didn't want to write out the answers to the questions, much less think about those answers. You probably had to be more emotionally vulnerable than you wanted to be, but I hope that vulnerability has allowed you to uncover new insight into who you have been, who you are now, and who you want to become.

While the benefits of the 4 STEPS have likely helped you break the addictive cycle, please know that until you get at the root cause(s) of your addiction, you could potentially get caught back up in that cycle. It isn't uncommon to fall back into the addictive cycle even after going through the 4 STEPS; in fact, that's just what I did. It takes practice to get to a place where you are consciously choosing to use the STEPS when you experience pain instead of turning to your addiction, as you have done in the past. The key is to understand what is at the root of your addiction. Until I realized that I hadn't accepted my sexuality and was trying to please the people I loved, I kept going back into the addictive cycle.

Another way to prevent a return to addictive behavior is to give to someone else or become a volunteer. By speaking and writing about my experiences as a former addict, my focus is no longer on finding a way to act out, but rather on helping others find ways to avoid acting out. As I mentioned earlier, I started the IT'S OK 2W8 (It's Okay to Wait) Campaign (www.itsok2w8.com), which challenges people to wait to have sex until they know their own and their partners' HIV and STD status. This campaign was a by-product of STEP 2. While STEP 2 is abstinence, the reality is that our youth were not practicing it. At the time the highest infection rates were among people who were in their teens and twenties. These are some of the ways I'm giving back and I'm challenging you to do something just as helpful, if not more so.

I sincerely hope that the 4 STEPS have helped removed some, if not all, of the layers that are covering up your pain. As I always say, "What you don't address, you can't change." If you know in your spirit you still have not gotten to the root of your pain, please seek insight from a professional. My therapist was able to get me to question beliefs that I vehemently defended, beliefs that were actually detrimental to me being happy and achieving my dreams. She got me to reflect on questions I had never wanted to think about; if she hadn't provoked me to do that, I never would have gained the insights I did. She challenged me to rethink certain situations and circumstances in my life from a different perspective; without those challenges, I would not have been able to grow, or to realize that not only could I have the family I wanted, with a man I loved, I wasn't going to go to hell because of it. Please don't let your own pride or someone else's beliefs prevent you from receiving valuable insight from a professional, insight that might help you live the life you want.

As I was writing this book, it helped me simply to review the 4 STEPS. Although I am no longer struggling with sex addiction, my life has been extremely stressful lately. Reviewing STEP 1 allowed me to check in and assess whether I was stressing over things God had called me to do, or just things I felt I needed to do in order to be successful. I realized that God has called me to reside in a place of peace, and that stress and peace don't inhabit the same space.

The 4 STEPS

Once I focused on STEP 1, it led me to examine the subsequent steps. I was able to look back on the way abstinence benefited my understanding of why I engaged in certain behaviors—STEP 2. From there I was able to reassess my life as it is now to see if I needed to jettison certain situations or people so I could draw in new energy or relationships—STEP 3. And, lastly, STEP 4: I realized how blessed I am to have a support network I can call on when I am stressed or just need some support.

The 4 STEPS is part of a toolkit I can use daily to help me stay focused and move in the direction of achieving my dreams and goals and helping others to achieve theirs. The 4 STEPS help me to remember that each of us is here on this earth for a purpose! And when I lose focus and become stressed, which can escalate into pain, I don't have to turn to an addiction to escape the pain.

At the end of the day, we all want to be loved and live a happy life. Knowing that God loves me as I am helps me to love myself and to let go of any stress or pain that comes up when I encounter people who don't love me as I am. **We have to manifest joy and happiness within before we can extend it to others. And we can't take in another's joy unless we can first feel it within ourselves.**

Conclusion

In closing, if you have found the 4 STEPS and this workbook helpful, please pass them along, perhaps to someone you know who is struggling with an addiction or is just discontent with life. The 4 STEPS can be helpful regardless of what a person is addicted to (sex, drugs, alcohol, gambling, food, etc.) or is struggling with. Whatever your race, sexuality, religious preference, aptitude, personality, or financial status, the 4 STEPS is intended for you. My culture and spiritual upbringing was based in the African-American Baptist Church, and so I write from a Christian perspective. Your perspective might be Muslim, Buddhist or Hindu: the benefits of the 4 STEPS are open to all. I wish you continued success in life, and I extend my greatest wish for your life: that you can and will achieve anything you put your mind to.

Acknowledgements

As always, I have to begin by thanking the Source of Love for all that He has done to help me complete this work. I'm continually amazed at how God brings thoughts, ideas, people and other resources in my life to help me accomplish things I could never do on my own. Thus, I have to next thank my parents, Dr. Eura Olivia Burks and Armistead Burks, Sr., for all their prayers, support and sacrifices throughout my journey. To my biological and extended family and friends, without your love and support I would not have been able to finish this workbook. Last but definitely not least, I want to thank certain individuals who provided an exceptional amount of support and/or played a critical role in The 4 STEPS: Belinda Anderson, Terry Thompson, Danyelle Godfrey, Alicia Alexander, Allyson Neal, Paul Guillory, Moses Mason, Xyna Bell, Ph.D., Mari Selby, August Tarrier, Ph.D., and Margie Baxley. Thanks again everyone and God's blessings and favor until the next one!

A.D. Burks

A.D. Burks, native Houstonian, author of Sex and Surrender: An Addicts Journey (www.sexsurrender.com) is a frequent guest on local and national talk/radio shows. Burks is a speaker and lecturer at local colleges, universities and community events. In an effort to prevent the increasing spread of HIV and STT's he founded the IT'S OK 2W8 (it's okay to wait) Campaign (www.itsok2w8.com). Burks holds a B.A. in Chemistry from Grinnell College and a M.A. in Business Administration from Rice University.

Want to share this GOOD NEWS with a loved one or friend? There are 2 ways to order your copy of

The 4 STEPS: A Practical Guide to Breaking the Addictive Cycle
A. D. Burks

1. Order directly from the publisher:
Burloc Media info@the4stepsguide.com

2. From Amazon.com

www.ingramcontent.com/pod-product-compliance
Lightning Source LLC
Chambersburg PA
CBHW060511100426
42743CB00009B/1280